D0927873

The 1983 Pere Marquette
Theology Lecture

THE THEOLOGY AND SETTING OF DISCIPLESHIP IN THE GOSPEL OF MARK

by
JOHN R. DONAHUE, S.J.

Professor of New Testament at the
Jesuit School of Theology and the
Graduate Theological Union, Berkeley

MARQUETTE UNIVERSITY PRESS
MILWAUKEE, WISCONSIN 53233

Library of Congress Catalogue Card Number: 83-060749

© Copyright 1983
Marquette University

ISBN 0-87462-538-6

Preface

The 1983 Père Marquette Lecture is the fourteenth in a series inaugurated to celebrate the Tercentenary of the missions and explorations of Père Jacques Marquette, S.J. (1637-1675). The Marquette University Theology Department, founded in 1952, launched these annual lectures by distinguished theologians under the title of the Père Marquette Lectures in 1969.

The 1983 lecture was delivered at Marquette University April 17, 1983 by Rev. John R. Donahue, S.J., Professor of New Testament at the Jesuit School of Theology and the Graduate Theological Union, Berkeley, CA.

Fr. Donahue studied theology at Woodstock College, MD, and New Testament at the University of Chicago, where he received his Ph.D. in 1972 under Norman Perrin. He has published *Are You the Christ? The Trial of Jesus in the Gospel of Mark* and a number of articles on the gospel of Mark in *The Passion of Mark,* and in *Interpretation* and the *Journal of Biblical Literature* and is preparing the *Hermeneia* commentary on Mark. He has lectured and written on other issues of biblical interpretation, especially in respect to contemporary theological and social concerns (e.g. "Divorce: New Testament Perspectives", "Biblical Perspectives on Justice" and "The Good News of Peace"). Along with Walter Brueggemann he is editor of the series *Overtures to Biblical Theology,* and has served for six years on the editorial board of the *Journal of Biblical Literature.*

Fr. Donahue has lectured extensively on the gospel parables, most recently at Union Theological Seminary in Richmond, and is preparing a book on the parables entitled, *Proclaiming the Gospel in Parable.* He has taught at Woodstock College, N.Y. (1972-73) and at Vanderbilt Divinity School (1973-1980) prior to coming to Berkeley. He has also lectured in the Theological Winter School in South Africa and Zimbabwe and as a visiting professor at the Pontifical Biblical Institute in Rome and Notre Dame University.

Introduction

More than twenty five years of study of the Gospel of Mark from the perspective of redaction criticism has revealed that it is a complex and significant theological work in the development of early Christianity. Since W. Marxsen's seminal essays in 1956 virtually every aspect of Mark's theology and the context of this theology have been examined.[1] This examination has proceeded in definite stages with Christology and Eschatology occupying the front stage. In recent years, however, the emphasis has shifted to the question of disciples and discipleship in Mark.[2] This interest in the Markan portrait of the disciples coincides with interest in the background to discipleship in the New Testament period and to examinations of discipleship in other New Testament works. It also coincides, especially in Roman Catholicism, with the adoption of discipleship as a broad theological and ecclesiological category which is evident in the description of the church as a "community of disciples" in the encyclical *Redemptor Hominis* by John Paul II and in the adoption of this phrase by Avery Dulles as a comprehensive model for the church.[3]

While a work which begins with the statement "the good news of Jesus, Messiah, Son of God," (Mk 1:1) has an obvious Christological thrust, with the sayings and deeds of Jesus in the forefront, the story of the disciples occupies a strong second position. In fact what is new about the form "gospel" are not new insights into Christology since the modes of Christology found in Mark are virtually all anticipated by the earlier Pauline letters. What is new is the narrative engagement of all kinds of people in the unfolding story of Jesus. The gospel of Mark tells us not only who Jesus is, but what it is to be involved with him. The structure of Mark vividly illustrates this.[4] Immediately after the initial proclamation of his mission, "The kingdom of God is at hand; repent and believe in the Gospel" (1:15), Jesus summons two pairs of brothers to follow him and to share in his mission (1:16-20). Every major section of the gospel begins with a story about discipleship and the middle section, 8:27-10:52, long recognized as the gateway to Mark's major theological concerns, consists almost completely of dialogue between Jesus and the disciples. The dramatic movement of the disciples from enthusiastic response to the call of Jesus through misunderstanding of his mighty works and teaching, especially of the necessity of his passion and death, and their final flight and denial involves the readers in examining what it means in their lives to follow Jesus. Mark's work is the proclaimed good news of Jesus; it is also the narrative of what it means to hear and to respond to this good news. [5]

In examining Mark's theology of discipleship and its setting, one must be a bit like the scribe of Matthew who brings from the storehouse things old and things new (Mt 13:51-52). Our aim is to present some of the major issues which have been of concern in the study of the disciples in Mark, to examine how Mark's distinctive theology of discipleship emerges especially in the narratives of the call and commissioning of the disciples and then to describe another set of texts which provide an entree to Mark's understanding of social interaction among Christians as a "community of disciples".

In addressing this task certain cautions emerge. Mark is one book which for Christians exists in the context of a canon of works with which they are to be in dialogue about their faith. From this one work cannot be derived a complete theology of discipleship. Also, many of those problems which are most intriguing in

Mark, such as the specific background to his understanding of discipleship, the relation of "the twelve" to the disciples and the enigma of the negative picture of the disciples, remain unsolved.[6] Nonetheless Mark *does* present the earliest sustained portrait of disciples and presents a foundation upon which Matthew and Luke build, even though their final edifices have distinctive shapes. Also as an independent book within the canon Mark has a distinctive shape and theology, to which very many people turn in our age to sustain their faith. Mark speaks about the reality of Christian life in stark and uncomprising lines. Unlike Matthew who speaks of those of "little faith" (Mt 6:30; 8:26; 14:31; 16:8), for Mark the choice is faith or lack of faith (4:40; 6:6). The response of those who come in contact with Jesus in Mark is most often that of fear, wonder or surprise.[7] The narrative pace of the gospel with its succession of uncomplicated sentences linked by "and" or "immediately" conveys an urgent tone to the story. Jesus dies with the words "My God, my God, why have you foresaken me?" (15:34); there is no resurrection appearance and the final words of the gospel are "they were afraid" (16:8). Mark summons readers to think about discipleship as an enterprise of utmost seriousness which involves standing before the mystery of God, a mystery both awe inspiring and enticing.[8]

Preliminary Problem

The Identification and Role of the Twelve

When describing those who respond to the call of Jesus and who "follow" him, Mark uses two principal terms, *hoi dōdeka,* the twelve (15 times), and *hoi mathētai,* the disciples (46 times).[9] The action of those who became companions of Jesus is described as "following" *(akolouthein),* for which there is no nominal equivalent in the gospels, or "coming after" *(elthein opisō),* both of which suggest active engagement in the task of a leader. Statistics, however, say little about the relative importance of the terms, especially of the twelve and the disciples. A host of problems surround them and one of the earliest monographs on Markan discipleship by Robert Meye centered on this problem.[10] The first and major problem is a literary one, the relation of tradition and redaction in "the twelve" texts. While Bultmann held that all references to the twelve are the "secondary editorial work of Mark," and may in part be due to a later copyist, Meye is at the opposite

end of the spectrum in claiming that all references are traditional.[11] The majority opinion as
presented most recently by Ernest Best holds
that the references to the twelve are a mixture of
tradition and Markan redaction, with the references in the Passion narrative, especially the
designation of Judas as "one of the twelve"
(14:10, 20, 43), holding the best claim to be tradition of the ministry of the historical Jesus.[12]

Allied to this literary problem is a historical
one: how does Mark stand in relation to other
early Christian views of the twelve? Two ori-
gins for the twelve are proposed, both rooted in
the "twelve tribe" symbolism of Israel.[13] One
view locates existence of the twelve in the eschatological consciousness and preaching of the
historical Jesus and adduces as evidence the Q
saying of Lk 22:29 (Mt 19:28), where those who
have followed Jesus are given assurance that
they "will sit on thrones judging the twelve
tribes of Israel." The disciples are thus thought
to be the eschatological nucleus of the new
people of God, the heir to the twelve tribes of
Israel. A second major theory draws on the
early resurrection *paradosis* of 1 Cor 15:3-7
which speaks of an appearance of Jesus to Peter
and the twelve. Here the twelve are seen to ori-
ginate not in the historical ministry of Jesus,

but in the consciousness of the community that the resurrection is the beginning of the new age and that the recipients of a resurrection appearance are the nucleus of a new community.

While the debate about the historical origin of the twelve continues, it is safe to say that Mark does not present a clear development of either of these traditions. In that very place where one would expect a saying like Lk 22:29-30, that is, in response to the request of John and James to sit at the right and left hand of Jesus in his glory (10:37), there is no mention that they will judge twelve tribes. Also Mark has no resurrection appearance to the twelve and even in that verse which is viewed by many scholars as a promise of such an appearance, the charge of the messenger is "go tell his disciples and Peter," *not* "the twelve and Peter."[14]

If then a significant number of twelve texts in Mark are redactional and if the twelve are not the eschatological nucleus of a new community, the question arises as to the theological meaning of the twelve texts. Before addressing this question directly two other observations are necessary.

First, as Best notes, "the twelve and the disciples are often interchangeable terms"[15]. In significant places where the twelve appear

Mark fails to distinguish them from other groups. After addressing the parable of the sower to a large crowd (4:1-9), in 4:10 Jesus begins a series of esoteric instructions on "the mystery of the kingdom of God" (4:11) to a group identified as "those about him, with the twelve". While the Greek of this text is ambiguous and its meaning debated, it seems clear that here the twelve are associated with a larger group. In 10:32 Jesus is on his way to Jerusalem and in rather quick succession three potentially different groups, the disciples, those who followed him, and the twelve are mentioned as being with him. Thus in two important places Mark seems to merge the twelve with a larger group. In other places the significance of the twelve seems reduced. Though the call and commissioning of the twelve occur at important places in the gospel (3:13-19; 6:6b-13), at other important places such as the transfiguration (9:2-8), the eschatological discourse (ch. 13) and Gethsemane (14:32-42), it is not the twelve who are present with Jesus but a smaller group of three or four. The only one of the twelve who is a "rounded" or developed character in the narrative is Peter who is also the only one who features prominently in the dialogues.[16]

Secondly, not only does Mark not single

out the twelve or distinguish them clearly from other groups, but there are a large number of other places where people, who are called explicitly neither the twelve nor disciples, do those very things the latter are called to do, to teach and do mighty works. [17] In 1:45 the healed leper begins to proclaim *(kēryssein)* many things and to spread the word *(ton logon* — used in Mark almost as an equivalent to gospel, cf. 4:13ff.) Many tax collectors and sinners follow *(ēkolouthoun)* Jesus (2:15), embodying the same response as those first called. The Gerasene demoniac begins to "proclaim" (5:20), as do the witnesses to the healing of the deaf and dumb man (7:37). An exorcist who is explicitly described as one who did not follow Jesus is "for Jesus" (9:38-40) and the blind Bartimaeus follows "on the way" (10:52) after the disciples fail to understand the necessity of suffering. A woman anoints Jesus for burial (14:1-9) and women accompany his body to the tomb (15:47) while a Jewish member of the council performs those burial rites which John's disciples do for him (15:42-46, cf. 6:29). Women first hear the message of the resurrection and are charged to carry it to the disciples (16:1-8). Clearly then Mark relativizes the significance of both the twelve and those explicitly called to be

disciples. In abstract categories, which though
foreign to Mark's realistic narrative are helpful
at the level of interpretation, we might say that
Mark moves in this fashion from a story about
disciples to a theology of discipleship.

If, then, for Mark the twelve are neither the
nucleus of the eschatological community, nor
does he identify discipleship with their response
and actions, what is their significance? Beginning
mainly with the work of Reploh who argued that
Mark was speaking through the past to the present of his community various suggestions have
emerged.[18] According to Klemens Stock the
twelve texts form a structural net over the whole
gospel and suggest a theological progression from
simply being called by Jesus to growth in a per-
sonal relation to him.[19] These texts thus provide
a concrete focus for a theology of discipleship
which is not to be limited to the historical twelve.
Another major importance of the twelve texts is
the strong missionary dimension of the narratives
in which they appear. Mark thereby roots the
missionary orientation of his community in the
period of its origin.[20]

I. The Call to Discipleship

The realization that discipleship is an important concern of Mark and that this is not

limited simply to the role of the twelve leads to engagement with Mark's understanding of what it means to heed the call of Jesus and to follow him. Ideally all those places where disciples or followers of Jesus are mentioned should be treated, but constraints of time preclude this. After some general remarks on the importance of discipleship pericopes to the structure of Mark and concerning the generally favorable picture of the disciples, we will select three narratives of the call and commissioning of disciples (1:16-20; 3:13-19; and 6:6b-13) as illustrations of the Markan theology of discipleship.

Discipleship pericopes have a very important function in the literary structure of the gospel.[21] After the prologue (1:1-15), the first public act of Jesus' ministry is the calling of disciples (1:16-20). Thereafter major sections and subsections of the gospel begin with discipleship pericopes. For example, the confession of Peter (8:27-30) initiates the major middle section of the gospel (8:27-10:52). The beginning of the Jerusalem ministry (chs. 11-13) is marked by a dialogue between Jesus and his disciples and this section concludes with the longest discourse of Jesus in the gospel, given to four disciples. The Passion narrative begins with a dual discipleship pericope, one the story of the woman

who anoints Jesus for death (14:1-9) followed by
a story of a false disciple, Judas (14:10-11), and
of disciples who prepare the upper room for
Jesus (14:12-16). The final words spoken by a
character in the gospel are a charge to the
women to deliver a message to his disciples and
Peter (16:7).

Despite the negative picture of the disciples
which we will shortly address, the general picture of them is positive. The disciples are the
constant companions of Jesus and the bulk of
the discourse material is between Jesus and the
disciples. He summons and commissions them
and gives them that *exousia* or power which the
Son of Man has (2:10, cf. 3:15; 6:7; 13:34).
They witness his mighty works (e.g. 1:21-34),
even those done apart from the crowd (1:29-30;
5:37-43), and, in accord with the root meaning
of the term *mathētēs* (one who learns from a
teacher), they receive not only Jesus' public
teaching but private instruction denied to
"those outside" (4:10-13; 33-34; 7:17ff.; 13:3ff.)
and, even though they misunderstand, the
coming passion, death and resurrection is dis-
closed to them (8:31-33; 9:31-32; 10:32-34). In
both feeding narratives he breaks the loaves
and gives them to the disciples to set before the
people (6:41; 8:7). In pericopes which are paral-

lel in both language and structure the disciples prepare the colt for the entry to Jerusalem and the upper room for the final meal (11:1-6; 14:12-16). Even though the disciples flee at his arrest (14:50), this has been divinely foreordained (14:27), and Jesus promises that after his resurrection he will meet them in Galilee (14:28, cf. 16:7).

Narratives of Calling and Mission of the Disciples

Mark 1:16-20: A Paradigmatic Call

This narrative forms the first of those narratives dealing with the vocation or mission of disciples which Stock notes form a structural web over the narrative and communicate the core of a theology of discipleship.[22] What has been called the "prologue" to the gospel of Mark, those introductory verses dealing with the ministry of John the Baptist, the baptism and temptation of Jesus (1:1-13), concludes with the separation of the ministry of Jesus from that of John by the arrest of John (1:14) and the beginning of Jesus' preaching in language which is significant for the theology of the whole gospel:

> After John was handed over, Jesus came into Galilee proclaiming the gospel of God and saying "the appointed time has come to pass, and the kingdom of God is at hand; repent and believe in the gospel" (1:14-15).[23]

Jesus is here portrayed as the eschatological herald of God's rule in history. A new *kairos* or period has come which calls forth a twofold human response, *metanoia,* conversion or change of heart, and *pistis,* belief or whole hearted commitment to the good news of God. The saying is a combination of the proclamation of gift (the time has come; the kingdom is at hand) and response (conversion and belief) and is meant to tell the reader how to enter into the whole gospel narrative which will unfold. We must always keep in mind that Mark is writing for people who have responded to the gospel so that he is not describing the conditions for discipleship, but its consequences.

In the narrative of the call of the first four disciples we find portrayed with the simplicity of a medieval woodcut the embodiment of what it means to respond to the proclamation of the kingdom. The language is reminiscent of the call of Elisha by Elijah and the two calls in this short pericope display a similar structure.[24] Jesus is in motion and encounters people in their ordinary activity (casting or mending of nets). The "call" is not precipitated by any request or activity by those called and is in the form of a command to which there is an immediate response. Unlike stories about rabbis and their disciples from roughly the same period in which the disciples seek out a rabbi and become disciples after long periods of training, in the Markan call narrative the initiative always comes immediately from Jesus.[25] The response to the call by Simon and Andrew and by James and John involves three elements: (a) they leave their occupation and family, (b) they follow after the one who calls — which Venerable Bede notes means "imitating the pattern of his life, not just walking after him,"[26] (c) and they are to be engaged in the work or mission of the one who calls, "I will make you fishers of men."

The rapid sequence of narratives which follow the call of the first four disciples portrays Jesus as one who offers "a new teaching in power" (1:28), who evokes wonder and admiration from the crowds. Various elements of tradition are incorporated by Mark to convey the initial impact of Jesus as one mighty in word and work. In addition to the miracles and exorcisms, Jesus also engages in a series of controversies (2:1-3:6) three of which, the defense of eating with tax collectors and sinners (2:16-17), the dispute over fasting (2:18-22) and over plucking grain on the Sabbath (2:23-28) involve Jesus in defending his disciples. Also in this first section the cross casts its shadow over the ministry of Jesus in the indication that the bridegroom will be taken away (2:20) and that the Pharisees and Herodians plot to kill Jesus (3:6).

Mark 3:13-19; The Call of the Twelve

After a Markan summary (3:7-13) which simultaneously concludes the first major part of the gospel and provides a transition to the second part, this second part, like the first, begins with the account of the "institution" of the twelve. The importance of the scene is indicated by its location on the mountain (3:13) and implied withdrawal of Jesus from the crowds.[27] Those elements of the call which were observed in 1:16-20 appear here with the difference that the "call" dimension is condensed while the mission aspect is expanded. The call is described simply by the phrase "he summoned those whom he wished." While condensed, this phrase captures both the unmediated and the gratuitous nature of the call found in 1:16-20. Likewise the response of those called is simply "they came to him" which suggests an equal immediacy of response. In the following verses the mission of the disciples is given in more explicit form than in the initial call narrative. First they are summoned "to be with him" (3:14) and secondly that he might send them out to preach and have power to cast out demons (3:15). The phraseology is awkward here with the change of persons (in order that *they* and that *he*) in the purpose clause. One would expect the text to read "that they might be with him and that they might preach, etc." The reading in the text thus stresses that mission originates with Jesus and that the "being with" Jesus is preparation for being sent out by Jesus. As in the case of the call of the first four, discipleship has a double focus, "being with" Jesus and doing the things of Jesus. This perspective is confirmed by the textually uncertain addition in 3:14 that those he appointed as the twelve, he also named "apostles."[28] Also, more explicit than in the call of the first four disciples is the incorporation of those called into a new social unit or group, "the twelve," with a new identity symbolized by the new names given to the first three listed, Simon, James and John, now to be called respectively, Peter and the sons of thunder.

6:6b-13: The Mission of the Twelve

This third and final call/commissioning narrative in Mark more explicitly than the first two stresses the missionary role of the twelve. Also very important is its context. The narratives between the "institution" of the twelve and their actual sending out picture that growing misunderstanding and division which the teaching and mighty works of Jesus will cause and culminate in the rejection of Jesus by his fellow townsfolk and relatives, and the characterization of their attitude as "lack of faith" (*apistia,* 6:6a). The twelve who will respond immediately to Jesus' command function as models of faith and at the same time form a new family around Jesus which is a substitute for the natural family.

The "call" is indicated simply by the same verb used in 3:13, *proskaleitai,* he summoned them (6:7). The mission aspect is the most developed of the three narratives. Jesus dispatches them as missionary pairs in language perhaps influenced by early Christian missionary practice (cf. 1 Cor 9:5-6). They are to live the life style of itinerant preachers and are given power over demons. Like Jesus they are to summon people to conversion, they are to expel demons and to heal the sick. In contrast to the projected missionary activity of 3:13-19, here Mark notes that the twelve actually engaged in such activity and will subsequently note that they returned and told Jesus all they had done and had taught (6:30).

Significance of the Call Narratives

While the call/commissioning narratives do not provide a complete theology of discipleship, and while they must be qualified by the negative picture of the disciples, they are significant in providing the basic elements of such a theology, both for the gospel of Mark and for subsequent reflection. The Jesus who speaks through the gospel to the Markan church is not a Jesus who lived in isolation. The first public act of his ministry was to summon disciples who were to follow him and to participate in his mission. Those first called are soon joined by others who form around Jesus a community which he empowers and instructs. In the call of the disciples the radically communitarian dimension of Christianity is vividly affirmed. Discipleship involves not simply hearing the summons of Jesus, but engagement with others who heed that same summons and embody a response to it in their lives. To "be with" Jesus is to be with others in community. Much of the subsequent unfolding of discipleship in Mark, together with the depiction of its pitfalls, will develop the implications of the meaning of this two-fold solidarity.

At the same time Mark's call narratives are a caution against a reductionism which would reduce an individual to a nameless face in a group. In Mark, though the call is to become a member of a group, it is not mediated or authorized by the group. The disciples are summoned by direct and immediate contact with Jesus, a summons which is freely given and independent of their previous status. Paul will express the same phenomenon by saying that the gospel he received was not "according to man" or "from man" but through a revelation of Jesus Christ (Gal 1:11-12). So too is the call to discipleship independent of the previous state of the one called. Mark depicts this in narrative form by indicating the variety of those called who comprise sons of a seemingly well to do owner of a fishing business (1:20, the sons of Zebedee leave their father and *hired servants*), people whose occupation places them at the margin of society (2:13ff., Levi and the tax collectors), and those who might have been religious zealots (3:18, the sons of thunder and Simon, the zealot). Again, Paul and later theology will express this in the more theological category of "grace" (see 1 Cor 15:10, "by the grace of God I am what I am"). Mark thus provides a grounding for the strain of theology which has always recognized that every individual stands before the mystery of God and that the workings of God with any person can not be reduced to institutional categories and institutional expectations.

Finally, both the individual and social dimensions of the call have an "apostolic" or missionary dimension. Neither the individual called nor the group is summoned to an interior spiritual quest divorced from that conflict and confrontation which proclamation of the gospel involves. The first public event after the call of the disciples in 1:16-20 involves Jesus' confrontation with the power of evil (1:21-28). After the call and commissioning of the twelve in 3:13-19 Jesus is judged by those of his company to be out of his senses and is accused by religious authorities of blasphemy (3:20-30), and the mission of the twelve in 6:7-13 is followed immediately by the account of the murder of John the Baptist, who, like Jesus, preaches and then is handed over (6:17-29). [29] "Being with" Jesus and doing the things of Jesus involves confrontation with the power of evil, false understanding and the possible loss of life in preparing the way for Jesus.

The Negative View of the Disciples

The first major section of Mark's gospel (1:1-8:26) provides the most sustained positive portrait of the disciples. Called and commissioned by Jesus they witness his miracles, participate in his saving power and are given the mysteries of the kingdom of God. Jesus defends them when they are attacked and comes to their rescue when they are in danger of being overwhelmed by the wind and the waves (4:35-41). At the same time those clouds begin to form on the horizon which will culminate in the flight of the disciples (14:50), the denial of Peter (14:66-72) and in the picture of an abandoned Jesus silhouetted on a cross against the darkened skies (15:33-35). The misunderstanding of the disciples is first hinted in 1:36 when Peter and those with him "track down" Jesus in the desert place where he retreats for prayer. After the disciples are given the mystery of the kingdom of God (4:10-12), Jesus explains that the parable of the sower means that some who receive the word will fall away for a variety of reasons (4:13-20). At the end of the first calming of the storm, Jesus says bluntly to the disciples: "Have you no faith?" (4:40). The disciples share with the crowd astonishment and amazement at the power of Jesus (e.g. 1:27; 4:41), and yet in 6:52 Mark states that "they did not understand about the breads for their minds were closed."[30] The disciples do not understand the teaching on the clean and unclean (7:18) and in 8:17-18 they are described as having hardened hearts and eyes which do not see and ears which do not hear, in terms very much like those used to describe the outsiders in 4:10-11. In the important middle section of the gospel, as virtually all commentators note, there is a pattern where three times Jesus predicts his death and resurrection (8:31; 9:31; 10:33) and three times the disciples fail to understand his teaching, but instead avoid any discussion of suffering (8:32) or begin to bicker about questions of precedence in the community (9:33-35; 10:35-40).[31] In the Passion narrative, after sharing a final passover meal with Jesus, the disciples sleep while Jesus struggles in the garden (14:32-42). Judas, one of the chosen twelve betrays him; all flee at his arrest and Peter denies him. In fact the last words spoken by a disciple in the gospel are not a confessional formula but an oath of denial, "I do not know this man about whom you are talking" (14:71). Some authors claim that even the women who follow Jesus to the cross and are the recipients of the resurrection proclamation (16:6) ultimately fail since they remain silent and fearful and do not deliver the message to the other disciples (16:7-8).[32]

These two rather discordant motifs of the positive and negative picture of the disciples which permeate Mark have spawned one of the more vigorous and creative debates in Markan scholarship over the last decade.[33] Mapping the contours of the debate would be beyond the bounds of the present discussion so we will indicate some of its major pathways and add a few comments on what we feel is "the positive significance of the negative picture of the disciples."

The most important (and controversial) positions are those of Theodore Weeden and Werner Kelber who build on many of the negative characteristics noted above but adduce different explanations of the data. Weeden notes in Mark a definite progression from unperceptiveness in 1:1-8:26 through misconception of Jesus' messianic role (8:27-10:52) to outright denial and rejection.[34] Behind this pattern Weeden sees a lively dispute in the Markan community caused by those who worship Jesus as a "divine man," a heavenly figure come to earth with supernatural power who promises his followers full participation in this power. According to Weeden Mark's strategy is to expose this theology as heretical by making the disciples in the gospel its exponents and portraying their failure as the consequence of such a theology. Thus Peter wants to remain in the glory of the transfiguration rather than follow Jesus on the way of the cross (9:5). By the harsh judgments Jesus utters against the disciples Mark exposes this theology and the lack of a resurrection appearance undercuts the claim of any group to have had privileged access to the presence of Jesus. The only proper Markan theology of discipleship is a willingness to accept fully the theology of the cross and to renounce any theology of power and glory.

Kelber's position builds on the same negative picture of the disciples observed by Weeden, but his view of the situation of the Markan community is more complicated. The heresy Mark combats is not primarily a Christological one, but an eschatological one.[35] From an analysis of chapter 13 Kelber argues that Mark was written after the destruction of the Jerusalem temple in AD 70. This destruction was claimed by the false prophets of 13:5-6, 21-22 to be the sign of the return of Jesus with whom they identified. Mark counters this heresy according to Kelber by putting on the

lips of the historical Jesus the proper eschatology of the kingdom. The kingdom which was
first preached in Galilee (1:14-15) will be
restored in Galilee (16:7-8) and the Markan
Christians are to look to Galilee as the place
where they will meet the risen Lord, at a new
time, still in the future, and not in Jerusalem
after the destruction of the temple.

While the disciples do not function, as in
Weeden's theory, as the immediate exponents
of this incorrect eschatology, their negative portrait is due to concerns of the Markan church.
Kelber links closely the disciples, especially
Peter, James and John with the relatives of
Jesus who in 3:21; 31ff., and 6:4-6 misunder-
stood Jesus.[36] Historically the Jerusalem
church was under the leadership of a relative of
Jesus, James, the brother of the Lord. Kelber
claims that this church had a distinct eschatology which the parousia deceivers of Mark's day
exploited. The claim to authority of the Jerusalem church is through natural relationship to
Jesus or through direct succession to the origi-
nal twelve. By discrediting both the relatives of
Jesus and the twelve, Mark discredits the authority of those in the Jerusalem church of his day
who propounded a false eschatology which
joined the coming of the kingdom with the

destruction of Jerusalem. It is the Markan Jesus who himself discredits their theology by pointing to his own return, not in Jerusalem, but in Galilee and at a time disassociated from the fall of Jerusalem.

To do adequate justice to these positions would take us too far afield. However, two remarks are in order. First, both theories are too dependent on a construct of Markan opponents for whom there is not adequate independent evidence. The model of Pauline opponents does not transfer easily to the genre gospel. Paul's letters contain explicit allusions to definite opponents (e.g. Gal 1:6-7; 2 Cor 11:12-15) and often quotations of their positions (e.g. 1 Cor 6:12; 8:1) and yet there is little assured consensus on any specific group of Pauline opponents.[37] Secondly, there have been a number of studies which take account of the negative picture of the disciples, but attribute this either to a theological concern of the Evangelist or explain it in terms of the literary dynamics of the narrative. Such an approach, they feel, provides a more secure ground for interpretation than a constructed social context. These authors can be subsumed under the rather paradoxical rubric of those who see the positive function of the negative role of the disciples in Mark.

Earlier studies, especially by Burkill and Luz, explained discipleship failure in terms of the messianic secret.[38] Since in Mark Jesus does not want his identity to be known until after the resurrection (9:9-10), it is understandable that the disciples would misinterpret Jesus' messiahship as a theology of glory instead of the way of the cross. Akin to this view is that of Quentin Quesnell that the disciples "illustrate how far from the natural man is the ability to grasp the things which are of God," and that the truths involved in understanding Jesus are "gifts of God for the reception of which one must be grateful."[39] Most recently Ernest Best has adduced a theological reason with implications for the community of Mark. According to Best, Mark *does not* reject the disciples but uses them as examples to teach his Roman community the true meaning of discipleship.[40] The failure of the disciples after initial enthusiasm, he argues, mirrors the stages of growth in faith in the community, that is, (1) faith attracted by the charismatic activity of church members and (2) developing under the challenge of suffering to a deeper faith where the cross is at the center of a true religious life.

Allied to these positions but slightly different is the position of Robert Tannehill,

followed in the main by Joanna Dewey and
Elizabeth Malbon — a group of scholars con-
cerned mainly with literary analysis of the text
rather than with its extra-textual referrents.[41]
For Tannehill the key to understanding the disciples in Mark lies in the dynamic interaction
between the reader and the text. The progression from positive following through rejection
and denial means that Mark tells a story in
which the reader is both to identify with the disciples and progressively to distance himself or
herself from them. The readers are summoned
to identify their own failures as disciples and
then to repent of them, so that the story of the
disciples becomes the narrative unfolding of the
command of 1:15, "be converted and believe in
the gospel."

While this array of positions which seek to
explain the failure of the disciples either in
terms of a polemic against opponents or as a
theological leitmotif of the narrative do not ad-
mit of reconciliation, some generalizations are
in order. The explanation of the negative role
of the disciples in terms of a vigorous polemic
against opponents in the Markan community
has not met with wide acceptance, not only
because of the difficulty of obtaining independent verification for such opponents, but more

strongly because such a polemic is difficult to reconcile with the strong positive theology of discipleship in Mark.[42] Those literary and theological explanations which assign a positive meaning to the negative picture while not yet providing a definite solution provide the way to fruitful reflection.

The discussion about the calls of the disciples as well as that about their negative and positive roles share one common feature. The picture of discipleship which emerges has a marked individualized cast. Even though the discussion is of a group or select individuals in a group (e.g., the four, the three, James and John), they all appear as single *dramatis personae.* The language used by contemporary authors is highly individualized and reflects a contemporary world view which often portrays the religious question of the autonomous individual before the mystery of God. However, as Bruce Malina has cogently argued in *The New Testament World: Insights From Cultural Anthropology,* such an individualized perspective is foreign to the first century Mediterranean world view which was characterized by the "dyadic personality," that is the individual in relation to a larger group.[43] So too, Markan studies with the exception of Howard Kee's important work,

Community of the New Age, have been bereft of examiniations of the communal dimension of discipleship in Mark, and even Kee's work stresses the social location of the community rather than its inner structure.[44] In the second major section of our study we will present some initial probings of this issue.

II. The Community of Disciples in Mark

To ask about Mark's understanding of discipleship in community is to speak about Mark's ecclesiology. However this task is made difficult not only by the lack of studies on this topic but by the absence in Mark of specifically ecclesiological language. Unlike Matthew (16:18; 18:17) and Luke (in Acts 8:1; 9:31, for example), Mark never uses the term *ekklēsia* and lacks the kind of incipient picture of church office which Matthew gives in the story of Peter (esp. 16:18-20) or Luke in the depiction of the authority of apostles (Acts 1:26; 2:42; 4:37). However, there is one set of related terms which Mark shares in common with other parts of the New Testament and which were very early used by the church to describe itself. By this I mean the language associated with house-

hold and family. In a recent study of 1 Peter,
John Elliott has shown the importance of this
language for understanding both the theology
and social setting of an important early Christian community.[45] At the same time he calls at-
tention to the lack of any systematic study of
the importance of household language in both
the New Testament as a whole and in specific
documents.[46] There has also been a resurgence
in New Testament studies dealing with early
Christian "house churches".[47] While a complete
study such as Elliott calls for is lacking in Mark,
and while, at this point, we will attempt no
such study, we will select four passages in Mark
where household language becomes a prism
through which we can see different shades of
Mark's understanding of discipleship as life in
community.

Mark 3:20-35:
The True Family of Jesus

This rather complex section of Mark consists of (a) an attempt by those of Jesus' company *(hoi par' autou)* to restrain him because they
think he is "beside himself" (3:20-21); (b) a
charge by scribes from Jerusalem that Jesus is
possessed by Beelzebul along with Jesus'

response to them in the parables of the divided
house and the divided kingdom and his pro-
nouncement that the sin against the Holy Spirit
is the unforgiveable sin (3:22-23) and (c) a
statement by Jesus on who constitutes his true
family (3:31-35). [48] What unites the sections is
the location of all three incidents in the house
mentioned in 3:20, as well as the use of household and family imagery (3:25; 32; 34-35). Also
the three sections mirror the familiar Markan
technique of intercalation where a narrative is
begun (3:20-21), only to be interrupted by
another narrative (23-30) and then resumed
(31-35) so that the two narratives interpret each
other. [49] The Jesus who is thought by his family
or close associates to be out of his mind and by
his opponents to be possessed is actually the
strong one. From 1:7 onward the reader knows
that Jesus is "the stronger one" predicted by
John, and the early exorcisms (esp. 1:21-28)
depict Jesus as one who despoils the kingdom of
Satan. This same Jesus as master of an undi-
vided household can determine who will be the
true members of his family. Thus the intercalation of the two narratives functions in the
service of Christology and discipleship. The
part of the section which most concerns us is the
response which comes in the third part when

the mother and brothers of Jesus are outside and seek him *(zētousin),* a term which in Mark generally has a pejorative connotation (3:32, cf. 1:37; 11:18; 12:12). When the crowd informs Jesus that his family is calling to him and seeking him, he replies, "And who are my mother and brothers?" Jesus then turns to the crowd sitting around him (the standard position for a disciple listening to a teacher) and says:

> Here are my mother and my brothers! Whoever does the will of God is my brother and sister and mother (3:34b-35).

An initial entree to the significance of this text is provided by the context of the whole section. The first major section of Mark concludes in 3:6 with the ominous hint of mortal opposition to Jesus. After a transitional summary about crowds streaming to Jesus (3:7-12), the second major section of the gospel (3:13--6:6), like the first, begins with a discipleship story, the installation of the twelve (cf. 1:16-20). The narratives and discourse which then follow deal with the breach which the deeds and teaching of Jesus will cause and the whole section culminates in the rejection of Jesus in his own country, among his own kin, and in his own house (6:4), which is then followed by the narrative of the sending of the twelve (6:7-13). We are thus presented with an interesting architectonic pattern:

A 3:13-19   Choosing of the twelve
B 3:20-35   Opposition to Jesus by close associates
             and picture of Jesus as one who forms
             new family
C 4:1-5:42   Sayings and deeds which manifest divi-
             sion expressed often in language of con-
             trast (4:1-8; 22; 30-34) or in expressions
             which evoke wonder or surprise (4:41;
             5:20; 5:42)
B' 6:1-6a   Opposition to Jesus by his family and
             kin
A' 6:7-13   Mission of the twelve

Therefore the context and relation of the saying
on the true family to other parts of the gospel
sheds light on its meaning. Jesus is the one who
calls those he wishes and his activity precipi-
tates opposition and rejection by his natural
family. However Jesus forms a new family
which will be constituted by those whom he explicitly calls (the disciples) as well as those who
gathered around him to hear his teaching and
are summoned to do the will of God and thus
become members of a new family.

At this point the Markan Jesus does not indicate what in the concrete doing the will of God
involves. In fact, despite the importance of this
saying, the concept of the will of God does not
feature significantly in Mark. However, in one
critical place Mark offers the key to what doing
the will of God involves and why it makes of one
a mother, brother or sister to Jesus. This place
is in Gethsemane immediately prior to those
events where the divisions Jesus causes will

come to a head in his final rejection by his own people and his abandonment by his disciples. In his agony Jesus prays: "Abba, Father, all things are possible to you; remove this cup from me; yet not what I will, but what you will" (14:36). Jesus is portrayed here fulfilling the conditions of discipleship which he himself has stated earlier in the gospel. The disciple is to pray to God with a faith which believes that God will bring about what is sought (11:23-24) and is to become like a little child in order to enter the kingdom of God (10:15). Here Jesus uses the familiar and familial language of a child to a father in addressing God as Abba, and as one to whom all things are possible. However the radical disposition of Jesus is to accept the will of God, even while praying that it could be otherwise. Therefore "doing the will of God" (in 3:34) and becoming a member of Jesus' family is in its most radical sense being willing like Jesus to accept even suffering and rejection as being willed by God. It is this which Peter fails to do in 8:32 which Jesus characterizes as "thinking human thoughts," not "the thoughts of God" (8:33). Solidarity with Jesus in suffering makes of one a brother, sister or mother to Jesus who himself is truly Son of God when he can address his father in faith and trust before his impending cross. Such solidarity also involves membership in a new human family, a perspective which emerges most clearly in the next text we will discuss.

Mark 10:29-31: The New Family

The interrelationship of household and family language, discipleship and suffering brings us to the second major text of Mark which sheds light on Mark's understanding of community. In response to the statement of Peter, "Lo, we have left everything and followed you," Jesus says:

> Truly I say to you, there is no one who has left house or brothers or sisters or mother or father or children or lands for my sake and for the gospel, who will not receive a hundredfold now in this time, houses and brothers and sisters and mothers and children and lands, with persecutions, and in the age to come eternal life (10:29-30).

As in the case of 3:31-35, this text must first be considered in its larger context and then its importance to the whole gospel can be assessed.

The overriding context of this passage is the great middle section of Mark, the transition between the Galilean ministry and the Jerusalem Passion (8:22-10:52). The section is structured geographically around references to Jesus being "on the way" (8:27; 9:33; 10:32) which

suggests both the way of Jesus to suffering and
death and the way of discipleship which he will
teach during this journey to Jerusalem. In content the bulk of the material which consists of
Jesus' instruction of his disciples and the brack-
eting of the whole section by two stories of Jesus
healing blind men (8:22-26; 10:46-52), the latter of whom tries to follow Jesus on the way
(10:52), suggest that Jesus in the intervening
sections is giving insight to blind disciples.[50]
The section is also structured around three passion predictions of Jesus (8:31; 9:31; 10:33)
followed by three misunderstandings on the
part of the disciples which evoke further instruction by Jesus. Despite the fact that many
commentators hold that the overarching theme
of this whole section is the necessity of suffering
and the failure of the disciples to understand
the message of the cross, it is actually only after
the first passion prediction that Jesus gives any
extended instruction on the necessity of taking
one's cross to become his follower (8:34-38).[51]
After the second and third passion predictions
the instructions are much more about the
demands of a life of service or *diakonia* in contrast to the squabbles of the disciples over positions of prestige. In fact the whole material between the second passion prediction and the

final words of Jesus in the section is bracketed between two sayings on such service, both addressed to the twelve and both capturing an essential component of discipleship in community for Mark:

| 9:35 | If anyone wants to be first of all, let that one be last of all and servant *(diakonos)* of all |
| 10:43-44 | Whoever wishes to be great among you, let that one be your servant *(diakonos)* and whoever wishes to be first among you, let that one be the slave of all |

Therefore the imagery of household service *(diakonia)* is to characterize the way of discipleship.[52]

The proximate context of 10:29-31 is at the conclusion of a long instruction on discipleship which follows the second passion prediction. Both H. W. Kuhn and R. Pesch, who have examined this section in detail, note that, especially in chapter 10, Mark has incorporated much traditional material which deals with the kinds of social concern manifest in other first century religious communities, e.g. questions of marriage and children, wealth and riches, rank and order in the community.[53] The section is a combination of a "manual of discipleship" and a "community rule".

The immediate context of the saying under consideration is the private instruction Jesus gives his disciples after the pericope of the rich young man (10:17-31). Here as in the rabbinic stories of masters and disciples a person comes to Jesus seeking knowledge of what must be done to achieve eternal life. Jesus responds by citing the commands of the Torah and the seeker responds that he has observed all these from his youth. Jesus then looks on him with love and invites him to sell all that he has, give it to the poor and then to follow him. Unlike those first called in 1:16-20 who left family and occupation to follow Jesus the young man goes away sad "for he had many possessions" (10:22). This refusal evokes from Jesus a statement on the virtual impossibility of the rich entering the kingdom of God (10:23). The disciples counter with a question about who can be saved and Jesus responds, "among God all things are possible" (10:27), a reaffirmation of the absolute gratuity of salvation. Not even discipleship (as in the case of Judas) assures salvation and not even a failure to respond to its summons precludes it. Then as in 8:32 Peter responds in a manner which shows that he has grasped only one aspect of the previous discussion. He exclaims, "Behold, we have left everything and followed you!" (10:28). Matthew's addition, "what then shall we have" (Mt 19:27) captures the spirit of Peter's question as the answer of Jesus in Mark implies, the one who leaves many possessions will have these in hundred-fold and will also receive that eternal life which the rich man sought by observing the law.

Leaving family and home to follow Jesus is a well established part of the tradition of the sayings of Jesus. In Q it appears in a more radical form with the command to hate members of one's own family and to neglect familial duties such as the burial of a father.[54] According to Gerd Theissen such sayings are preserved by "wandering charismatics," a branch of the Jesus movement which combined an itinerant life style with a revolutionary élan which rejected the ethos of ordinary settled life.[55] Mark shows contact with such a tradition in the charge to the disciples in 6:7-13 to travel without bread or money and to move from place to place. However in 10:29-30 we find interesting variations of the motif.

First Mark is alone in joining to the command to leave one's family the promise of a new family described as the hundredfold "now in this time *(kairō)*"; Matthew, who follows Mark closely at this point, simply says that such people will receive a hundredfold (Mt 19:29), and Luke states simply that they will receive "manifold more" (Lk 18:30). While all three Evangelists promise eternal life, only Mark states that the family which has been left behind will be replaced by a new family. The hundredfold which the Markan reader knows from 4:20 is the fruit of hearing and doing the word of God is a new family based not on natural kinship but on the power of God. Such language should not be considered merely as a metaphor since in the early church the sense of community was expressed in familial language. Paul speaks of Onesimus as his child (Philemon 10) and tells the Corinthians that he became their father through the gospel (1 Cor 4:15). He compares his work among the Thessalonians to a nurse caring for children (1 Thess 2:7), and calls the mother of Rufus his mother (Rom 16:13).

Second, while the second part of the saying, the description of the new family, parallels the first part in virtually every detail, there is a significant omission.[56] Though the disciple is said to leave "mother or father", the disciple will receive "brothers, sisters, mothers and children." Expected but omitted is the reception of a new father. Possible explanations for this would be that for Mark the only father is God whom both the Christian community and Jesus are to address as such in prayer (11:25; 14:36, cf. Mt 23:9). Equally possible is that the Markan version of the statement embodies an "anti-patriarchal" stance and indicates the radically egalitarian nature of the Markan community, a perspective which is in tune with the general context of 9:30-10:45.[57] Mark's community is one where people are to be last of all and servants of all (9:35; 10:42-45), where children, who often symbolize the powerless, are to be accepted and embraced (9:36; 10:13-16), where husbands and wives cannot treat each other as property to be discarded (10:1-12) and where wealth and the social divisions it causes make it virtually impossible to enter the kingdom (10:17-27). Mark's new family is to be characterized by the renunciation of dominating power and by mutual service.

The final element of this saying which evokes comment is the curious addition of "with persecutions" *(meta diōgmōn)* to the new family. In form the phrase breaks the rhythmic parallelism of the verse and in content it relativizes the reward of the new family. One rather convincing explanation is that Mark wants to convey that one who leaves family for Jesus' sake and for the sake of the gospel will necessarily be involved in following the way of the cross.

Another intriguing explanation is offered by the literary analysis of Rober Tannehill.[58] He views the addition as an ironic joke. The reader is said to be caught up in the prospect of rewards which far exceed the sacrifice. The addition creates a humorous incongruity which like all jokes debunks our pretensions by suggesting that the final reward (the hundredfold) does not absolve one from engagement with the contingencies of history (persecution).

While both these explanations have much to recommend them and provide an example of a text with multiple interpretations, we would like to propose a less theological or literary interpretation which reflects the realities of Mark's community. The conjunction of the new family with persecution is in accord with other statements in Mark about family relationships. As we have seen in 3:20-35 it is misunderstanding between Jesus and his natural family which evokes Jesus' statement that the new family is constituted not by natural ties, but by doing the will of God. In 6:1-6, Jesus is himself rejected by his own kin and household. In the eschatological sermon of Mark 13, which may mirror actual recent experiences of the community, one of the sufferings is that "brother will deliver up brother to death, and the father his child, and children will rise up against parents and have them put to death" (13:12). [59] For Mark, life in the new community involves very often persecution by the old.

We would also suggest that this juxtaposition of family and persecution sheds light on the social setting of the Markan community. John Elliott has shown in the case of 1 Peter that household language is a key not only to the ideology or self-definition of a community but to its actual situation. [60] Elliott stresses the positive aspect of this in terms of the internal strength and coherence it gives the community. Mark's use of household language serves a similar function or "strategy" (to use Elliott's terminology). It also indicates one of the reasons why the new family may have evoked persecution.

At this period Jewish, Hellenistic and Roman perceptions of family life are quite conservative. Strong family bonds were supported not only by social pressure but by a host of laws governing marriage, inheritance and the relation of different members of the natural and extended family. The power of the head of the family *(patria potestas)* was a virtual law unto itself. [61] A Christian community which evokes a saying of Jesus to claim that doing the will of God is more important than loyalty to the natural family and which actually counsels leaving the family to form a new family without the governing power of the father and which rejects those structures of interrelationship which govern normal family life would naturally evoke suspicion and persecution. Stephen Benko suggests that the statement of Tacitus (*Annals* 15:44) that Christians were persecuted during the time of Nero because of "their hatred of the human race" meant that for Tacitus Christians were a disruptive social phenomenon.[62] Paul Keresztes suggests that the phrase meant "the dereliction of one's duties toward the community of men, a separation from the rest of society."[63] A second century anti-Christian author complains that Christians love each other almost before they know one another and that they call each other promiscuously brother and sister.[64] Leaving parents, abandoning occupations and the pursuit of wealth, observance of Jesus' teaching on divorce, consideration for children — all these would bring Christians into conflict with the prevailing ethos and values and evoke that kind of suspicion and hatred which meant that the possession of new mothers, brothers and sisters would exist only "with persecutions."

Mark 10:42-45:
A Community of Service

The third text which offers insight into Mark's understanding of discipleship in community comes at the end of the middle section. After the third passion prediction, the disciples again engage in a dispute over power and precedence, in this case, James and John request positions of authority with Jesus "in your glory" (10:37). Jesus responds (as so often in Mark) with a counter question asking them whether they are prepared to follow him on the way of suffering. James and John respond that they are and Jesus predicts their future martyrdom, but says that it is not his to grant positions of power and authority but these are for those for whom such positions are prepared by God (10:40).[65] Rather subtly, the Markan Jesus responds to a question about power and glory by stating his own limitation in face of God's plan. This part of the discussion then concludes.

In the second part of the dialogue the other ten are indignant at the request of James and John, manifesting that same concern for power and precedence which appeared in 9:34. Jesus then responds in three sayings which sum up both the ethics and Christology of the whole

middle section of Mark. In the first saying
(10:42-43a) Jesus contrasts the expected behavior
of his followers with those who are supposed to
rule over Gentiles and lord it over them, and
with their great men who exercise authority. It
shall not be so among Christians. Jesus thus rejects the mode and manner in which power is ex-
ercised in the surrounding environment as ac-
ceptable in a community of disciples. The second
saying describes the way precedence and
authority is to exist in the community: "whoever
would be great among you must be your servant
(diakonos) and whoever would be first among
you must be the slave of all" (10:43b-44).

The use of servant *(diakonos)* to characterize
Christian behavior provides the point of contact between this section and the household/
family theme. Though it is used figuratively
and even becomes a term for an office in early
Christianity (Phil 1:1), *diakonos* never loses its
root meaning of a table servant or household
lackey.[66] This Markan perspective on mutuality rather than dominance is in contrast to other
religious communities of the time. For example
at Qumran there was great concern for precedence and the proper seating of leaders of the
community at the communal meals.[67] Paul indicates that one of the problems at Corinth

seems to be that important people in the community manifested their power in the way they celebrated the Lord's supper (1 Cor 11:17-34). Mark's image of the community leaders as table servants rather than those sitting at the places of honor is a clear affront to the social norms of the time and again conveys the radically egalitarian ethos of the Markan community.

The final saying of Jesus in this section, "For the Son of Man came not to be served but to serve and to give his life as a ransom for many," picks up this language of table service but extends it to an understanding of his whole life and crystallizes the meaning of suffering which has permeated this section. As the reader knows from 2:10 Jesus is the Son of Man who possesses authority on earth. As Son of Man he will suffer, die and be raised up (8:31; 9:31; 10:33) and as such he will come in glory (8:38). [68] And yet this same Son of Man is to be the servant who performs the ultimate service by giving his life that others may be free (a ransom for many). [69] For Mark, then, the ethics of discipleship is possible only when combined with a Christology of redemptive liberation. The community is one which has been freed by Jesus, but freed for a deeper level of mutual service done in solidarity with Jesus who by the paradoxical renunciation of power became the source of liberation for others.

Mark 13:33-36:
A Watchful Community

The final use of Markan household language which we will treat provides a brief underscoring of the perspective we have developed. At the end of the long eschatological discourse of chapter 13, Mark appends two parables which tell his church how to live during the period prior to the return of Jesus.[70] The certainty of the end is as assured as the coming of summer follows the spring budding of the fig tree (13:28-29). However only the Father knows the exact time or hour and in the intervening time the Christian posture is to watch (13:32-33). The final verses of the discourse are a virtual allegory of life in the Markan community. Their life is that of servants who are waiting for a master to return (13:34-36). The man who goes on a journey leaves his house *(oikian)* and gives to his servants *(doulois)* authority *(exousia)* and an assigned task *(ergon)*. The posture of the whole community waiting for the return of the "lord of the house" *(kyrios tēs oikias)* is watchfulness, that is active waiting.

Behind this allegorical language are clear references to the situation of the Markan church. We have already seen that the community are to be servants of each other (10:43-44). Like the servants in the parable the disciples of Jesus possess the *exousia* which he gives (6:7). The community exists in a period between the resurrection and the parousia of Jesus, which the parable describes as the return of the "lord of the house". We would claim that this allegory reflects the experience of a Markan house church, assembled in mutual service and watchfulness which recognizes only Jesus as the lord of the house and waits for his return.

Conclusion

Study of the general picture of the disciples in Mark, of their calls and commission and of their life in community expressed in the language of house and family, enables us to make some generalizations about discipleship in Mark. In so doing we must always keep in mind that Mark is writing a gospel, good news, not an ethical treatise. He is writing principally for believers and describing the consequences of discipleship, not its conditions. Mark presents a narrative picture of the implications of the faith they share with each other and the engagement with the mystery of Christ which results from their baptisms. As such Mark is a narrative expansion of the journey of commitment and recommitment that is to characterize Christian life.

Such a life is to hear again the proclamation of Jesus, "be converted and believe in the good news" (Mk 1:15). To believe, however, is to be called by Jesus in the midst of one's ordinary activity, to leave an old way of life and to follow a new path of companionship with Jesus and with others who have heard this call. The call is also an empowerment for mission and a life doing the things of Jesus. To share the life of Jesus in its most radical dimension involves trust in God even in the midst of undeserved suffering and a willingness to give one's life so that others may be free. Those who are called must be ready to leave old sources of identity and security, family and possessions, but will become members of a new family. This new family will be characterized by mutual service and the renunciation of the desire for power and prestige which is the way of the gentiles and not of the Son of Man.

We would claim that such a vision of discipleship was for Mark not simply an ideal, but was meant to describe the religious life of his house churches. While at this point the exact setting of Mark's theology of discipleship can not be specified, we would claim that it is in a house church that the Markan Christians live out their story of Jesus, Mark's good news. It is a community trying to be hearers and doers of the word (4:20). It is also a community which recognizes the good news of Jesus as its sole authority. Those who attempt to appropriate the authority of Jesus are called "deceivers" (13:6, 21-22). The immediacy of the calls to discipleship suggests an immediacy in the relation of the Christians to the absent "lord of the house" (13:35). Mark's community seems to be radically egalitarian in nature and the only visible structure of authority seems to be that of mutual service. At the same time it is not a sectarian community dedicated only to inner nurture. The one called to be with Jesus is also called to mission. The members of Mark's church, like Jesus, are to break down the barriers between Jew and Gentile.[71] Exclusivism is also to be avoided. The one who is not against Jesus is for him and the stranger who gives a drink of water will receive a reward. The major ethical posture of the community is the twofold command of love of God and of neighbor (12:28-34).[72]

Mark's vision of discipleship has a dual setting. The primary one is the historical setting where as prophet and pastor Mark brings the teaching of Jesus and the traditions of his church to bear on the concerns of the community. Mark's understanding of discipleship and life in community seems not to have had a great influence. As we have noted, Matthew and Luke alter Mark's picture of community life, as characterized by solidarity, mutuality and service, by showing more concern for issues of institutionalized authority and ministry. In later New Testament books such as Colossians, the Pastorals and 1 Peter household language is used to support structured authority and subordination, rather than to describe a situation in which those in authority are to be ministers (*diakonoi*) and servants (*douloi*) as in Mark.[73] While such a development may mirror a necessary stage in the evolution of a religious movement or may reflect varied responses of diverse groups to different social pressures, it does stand in tension with Mark's vision.

Mark's work also has a setting in the canon of the Christian scriptures. In canonizing Mark as an independent book the church sanctioned a dynamic and prophetic vision of discipleship and community which stands in tension with other New Testament perspectives and with that very institutionalized ethos out of which canonization emerges. To return to Mark's story of discipleship is not simply to recapture the experiences of a transient New Testament Community, it is to recapture a picture of Jesus and what it means to respond to his call which the church says should never be forgotten or glossed over by other more appealing or more relevant pictures.

Finally, Mark speaks not simply as prophet and pastor, but as poet, a maker of meaning and a shaper of worlds. Hugh Kenner has written of poets:

> Whoever can give his people better stories that the ones they live in is like the priest in whose hands common bread and wine become capable of feeding the very soul. [74]

Mark told his church a story which fed their very souls when they met in memory of him who took bread and said, "this is my body" (14:22) and said that a cup of wine was his covenant blood to be poured out for many (14:24). This story was a story better than the stories of war, of family betrayal and of profanation of the Holy City which shaped their lives (13:3-13). It was a story of being called by Jesus, of walking with him, of experiencing his love even amid failure and denial and of solidarity with others who were trying to hear the same story. It is our task today as a community of disciples to hear again Mark's old story and to transform it by our lives into a story for our age better than the ones people live by. Such transformation into an individual and community style of life based on Mark, which renounces the striving for prestige and power over others, and at the same time confronts the evil forces which oppress our society will bring with it suffering and persecution, as it did for John, for Jesus and for Mark's community. And yet this is not the final word. To hear the final word we must take our stand with the women before the door of death, now emptied of its power and hear again "he is not here; he is risen (16:6)."

Footnotes

1. *Der Evangelist Markus* (FRLANT, N.F., 68; Göttingen: Vandenhoeck und Ruprecht, 1956). Two helpful surveys of work done since Marxsen are: H. Kee, "Mark's Gospel in Recent Research," in *Interpreting the Gospels,* ed. J. L. Mays (Philadelphia: Fortress, 1981) 130-147 (originally published in *Int* 32 [1978] 353-368) and J. Kingsbury, "The Gospel of Mark in Current Research," *RelSRev* 5 (1979) 101-07.

2. The major monographs on Markan discipleship (in chronological order) are: R. P. Meye, *Jesus and the Twelve;*

Discipleship and Revelation in Mark's Gospel (Grand Rapids: Eerdmans, 1968); S. Freyne, *The Twelve: Disciples and Apostles* (London: Sheed and Ward, 1968); K.-G. Reploh, *Markus — Lehrer der Gemeinde* (SBM, 9; Stuttgart: Katholisches Bibelwerk, 1969); G. Schmahl, *Die Zwölf im Markusevangelium* (Trier: Paulinus, 1974); K. Stock, *Die Boten aus dem Mit-Ihm-Sein* (AnBib, 70; Rome: Biblical Institute, 1975); E. Best, *Following Jesus: Discipleship in the Gospel of Mark* (JSNT, Sup. 4; Sheffield: JSOT Press, 1981).

3. A. Dulles, "Imaging the Church for the 1980's," *Catholic Mind* 79, n. 1357 (1981) 8-26. Dulles cites *Redemptor Hominis* (n. 21) on p. 14.

4. Stock, *Boten,* 177; E. Schweizer, "The Portrayal of the Life of Faith in the Gospel of Mark," in *Interpreting the Gospels,* 168-182 (originally published in *Int* 32 [1978] 387-399).

5. On the interplay of narrative and theology in Mark see the fine studies by R. Tannehill, "The Disciples in Mark: The Function of a Narrative Role," *JR* 57 (1977) 386-405 and "The Gospel of Mark as Narrative Christology," *Semeia* 16 (1979) 57-95.

6. We will treat briefly the question of the twelve and of the negative role of the disciples. On the question of background see esp. H. D. Betz, *Nachfolge und Nachahmung Jesu Christi im Neuen Testament* (BHT, 37 Tübingen: Mohr [Siebeck] 1967); M. Hengel, *The Charismatic Leader and His Followers* (tr. J. Grieg; Studies of the New Testament and its World; New York: Crossroad, 1981); V. K. Robbins, "Mark 1.14-20: An Interpretation at the Intersection of Jewish and Graeco Roman Traditions," *NTS* 28 (1982) 220-236.

7. For example, after the miracles of Jesus (1:27; 2:12; 4:41; 5:15, 20, 33, 42; 6:50, 51; 7:37); as a reaction to Jesus' teaching (1:22; 6:2; 10:24, 26; 11:18; 12:17); in narratives of divine epiphanies (4:41; 6:50-51; 9:6; 16:5); in reaction to Jesus' prophecy of future suffering (9:32; 10:32); and in reactions of opponents of Jesus (11:18; 12:12; 15:5, 44).

For a fuller discussion of the significance of this phenomenon see, J. Donahue, "Jesus as the Parable of God in
the Gospel of Mark," in *Interpreting the Gospels,* 148-167
(originally published in *Int* 32 [1978] 369-386).

8. Readers may recognize in my formulation the influence
of R. Otto *The Idea of the Holy* (London: Oxford University, 1957).

9. Statistics are based on R. Morgenthaler, *Statistik des
Neuentestamentlichen Wortschatzes* (Zürich und Frankfurt:
Gotthelf Verlag, 1958).

10. *Jesus and the Twelve* (see n. 2 above).

11. R. Bultmann, *The History of the Synoptic Tradition* (tr. John
Marsh; New York: Harper and Row, 1963) 345; R.
Meye, *Jesus and the Twelve,* 228, followed by William
Lane, *Commentary on the Gospel of Mark* (The New Interna-
tional Commentary on the New Testament; Grand
Rapids: Eerdmans, 1974) 132.

12. E. Best, "Mark's Use of the Twelve," *ZNW* 69 (1978)
11-35.

13. For an excellent summary of the different positions on the
origin of the twelve see, G. Schmahl, *Die Zwölf,* 1-15.

14. As 3:13-19 shows and the very number suggests Mark
probably knows of twelve as a symbolic number for the
tribes of Israel, but he does not develop this significantly
for his theology. For an opposite opinion see, R. Pesch,
Das Markusevangelium (2 vols.; HTKNT 2; Freiburg/
Basel/Wien: Herder, 1976-77) 1. 205.

15. "Mark's Use of the Twelve," 35.

16. On characterization in Mark see, D. Rhoads and D.
Michie, *Mark As Story* (Philadelphia: Fortress, 1982)
122-29.

17. E. Schweizer, "The Portrayal," 172-173; R. Tannehill,
"Disciples," 404; J. Donahue, "A Neglected Factor in
Mark's Theology," *JBL* 101 (1982) 582-585.

18. See n. 2 above. Though Reploh's insight is commonplace
now, when it was presented it represented a significant
shift in the way Mark was read.

19. *Boten,* esp. 177, 185.

20. The strongest advocate of the missionary importance of the twelve is R. Pesch, for whom the gospel of Mark is primarily a *Missionsbuch.* See *Markusevangelium,* 1. 205, 67 (on missionary stress of Mark).

21. There has emerged a consensus on the major structural divisions of Mark. I am following the structure proposed by N. Perrin in *The New Testament: An Introduction* (2nd rev. ed. by N. Perrin and D. Duling; New York: Harcourt, Brace, Jovanovich, 1982) 243-254. This structure is very similar to that proposed by E. Schweizer, "Portrayal," 169, and by R. Pesch, *Markusevangelium,* 1. vii-x.

22. See n. 19 above.

23. On the importance of this whole passage as concluding the prologue of Mark see, L. Keck, "The Introduction to Mark's Gospel," *NTS* 12 (1966) 352-370. On its significance for the whole gospel, see W. Egger, *Frohbotschaft und Lehre: Die Sammelberichte des Wirkens Jesu im Markusevangelium* (Frankfurter Theologische Studien, 19; Frankfurt: Knecht, 1976) 46-64.

24. 1 Kings 19:19-21; R. Pesch, *Markusevangelium,* 1. 111.

25. On disciples and rabbis see, K. Rengstorf, *"mathētēs,"* *TDNT* 5. 431-440; J. Neusner, *First Century Judaism in Crisis* (Nashville: Abingdon, 1975) 95-114.

26. Hom. 21, *Corpus Christianorum, Series Latina* (Turnhout: Brepols, 1955--) 122, n. 149. Bede also has one of the few pre-modern commentaries on Mark.

27. W. Lane, *Mark,* 132. The mountain is the site of revelation and redemption in the Old Testament.

28. The text as edited both by the United Bible Societies (3rd ed) and by Nestle-Aland (26th ed.) retains the clause *hous kai apostolous ōnomasen* but places it in brackets. Though it has good manuscript evidence (e.g. Sinaiticus and Vaticanus), it is suspected of being an interpolation from Lk 6:13. See, B. Metzger, *A Textual Commentary on the Greek New Testament* (London/New York: United Bible Societies, 1971) 80.

29. N. Perrin, *The New Testament,* 238.

30. An exhaustive treatment of the significance of this difficult verse in Mark is offered by Q. Quesnell, *The Mind of Mark* (AnBib, 38; Rome: Biblical Institute, 1969).

31. N. Perrin, *What is Redaction Criticism?* (Philadelphia: Fortress, 1969) 40-56.

32. Among those who claim that the message is not delivered (and that there is no reconciliation between Jesus and the failed disciples) are: N. Perrin, *The Resurrection According to Matthew, Mark and Luke* (Philadelphia: Fortress, 1977) 31; T. J. Weeden, *Mark: Traditions in Conflict* (Philadelphia: Fortress, 1971) 47-50; 102-11; and N. Q. Hamilton, "Resurrection Tradition and the Composition of Mark," *JBL* 84 (1965) 415-421.

33. An early study is J. Tyson, "The Blindness of Disciples in Mark," *JBL* 80 (1961) 261-268. The negative view of the disciples is most associated with the following works: T. J. Weeden, *Mark: Traditions in Conflict* and "The Heresy That Necessitated Mark's Gospel," *ZNW* 59 (1968) 145-158; "The Conflict Between Mark and His Opponents Over Kingdom Theology," *Society of Biblical Literature 1973 Seminar Papers II* (ed. G. MacRae; Cambridge, MA.: SBL, 1973) 203-241; W. Kelber, *The Kingdom in Mark: A New Place and A New Time* (Philadelphia: Fortress, 1974); "The Hour of the Son of Man and the Temptation of the Disciples," in *The Passion in Mark* (ed. W. Kelber; Philadelphia: Fortress, 1976) 41-60; *Mark's Story of Jesus* (Philadelphia: Fortress, 1979); K. Dewey, "Peter's Curse and Cursed Peter," in *Passion in Mark,* 96-114. Opposed to this view strongly are the authors of *Peter in the New Testament* (eds. R. Brown; K. Donfried; J. Reumann; New York: Paulist; Minneapolis: Augsburg, 1973) 61-73.

34. *Traditions,* esp. 26-51; 159-168. Weeden's summary of his position which we follow here.

35. Kelber, *Kingdom,* esp. 82-84; 109-128; 138-145, Kelber's summary.

36. *Ibid.* 26, 53-55. See also, D. Crossan, "Mark and the Relatives of Jesus," *NovT* 15 (1973) 81-113, opposed by J. Lambrecht, "The Relatives of Jesus in Mark," *NovT* 16 (1974) 241-258.

37. For a good popular survey of different positions on Paul's opponents see, C. Roetzel, *The Letters of Paul. Conversations in Context* (Atlanta: John Knox, 1975). The most influential work in the modern discussion has been D. Georgi, *Die Gegner des Paulus im 2. Korintherbrief* (WMANT, 11; Neukirchen-Vluyn: Neukirchener Verlag, 1964).

38. T. A. Burkill, *Mysterious Revelation* (Ithaca, NY: Cornell University, 1963); U. Luz, "Das Geheimnismotiv und die Markanische Christologie," *ZNW* 56 (1965) 9-30.

39. *The Mind of Mark,* 170.

40. *Following Jesus,* 136-137.

41. R. Tannehill, see articles listed in n. 5 above and his more popular presentation, *A Mirror For Disciples: A Study in the Gospel of Mark* (Nashville: Discipleship Resources, 1977); J. Dewey, "Point of View and the Disciples in Mark," *Society of Biblical Literature 1982 Seminar Papers* (ed. K. Richards; Chico, CA: Scholars Press, 1982) 97-106, and her more popular, *Disciples of the Way: Mark on Discipleship* (Women's Division, Board of Global Ministries, United Methodist Church: n.p., 1976); E. Malbon, "Disciples/Crowds/Whatever: A Markan Narrative Pattern," Paper presented to the Society of Biblical Literature, Annual Meeting, Dec. 21, 1982.

42. Recently stressed by F. J. Moloney, "The Vocation of the Disciples in the Gospel of Mark," *Salesianum* 43 (1981) 487-516, esp. 492-93.

43. (Atlanta: John Knox, 1981) 60; see also his, "The Individual and the Community — Personality in the Social World of Early Christianity," *BTB* 9 (1979) 126-138.

44. Full title: *Community of the New Age: Studies in Mark's Gospel* (Philadelphia: Westminster, 1977).

45. *A Home for the Homeless. A Sociological Exegesis of 1 Peter: Its Situation and Strategy* (Philadelphia: Fortress, 1981) 165-266.

46. *Ibid.* 165, "The need for a comprehensive up-to-date study of *oikos* in the New Testament in general has long been recognized, but has yet to be met." In the case of Mark see a brief treatment by J. Schreiber, *Die Theologie des Vertrauens* (Hamburg: Furche, 1969) 161-164, and by E. Best, *Following Jesus,* 226-229. The most extensive treatment of house (and other spatial designations in Mark) is in the fine dissertation of Elizabeth Malbon, "Narrative Space and Mythic Meaning: A Structural Exegesis in the Gospel of Mark" (Unpublished PhD dissertation: Florida State University, Tallahassee, 1980). Using categories taken from Levi-Strauss, Malbon studies house in opposition to temple and synagogue, see 196-228. She criticizes my statement that in 14:58 Mark points to the community as the "temple not made with hands" (See, J. Donahue, *Are You The Christ? The Trial Narrative in the Gospel of Mark* [SBLDS, 10; Missoula: Scholars Press, 1973] and "Temple, Trial and Royal Christology (Mark 14:53-65)" in *The Passion in Mark,* (61-79). In formulating the positions of the present essay I have been influenced by her criticisms and her research. However, I would still hold that Mark may point to the new temple as a comprehensive symbol for his community and at the same time think of his church as a house church. Also "house" and "temple" are closely allied in biblical thought, and the community of 1 Peter provides an example of a group which used images from both the household (4:7-11) and the temple (2:4-10) to define itself.

47. To the early (and often overlooked) study by F. Filson, "The Significance of the Early House Churches," *JBL* 58 (1939) 105-112, add, R. E. Brown, "New Testament Background for the Concept of Local Church," in *The Catholic Theological Society of America. Proceedings of the Thirty-Sixth Annual Convention,* 36 (ed. L. Salm; New York: CTSA, 1982) 1-14, and H.-J. Klauck, *Hausgemeinde und Hauskirche im frühen Christentum* (SBS, 103; Stuttgart: Katholisches Bibelwerk, 1981).

48. On the complicated tradition history of this section, see R. Pesch, *Markusevangelium,* 1. 209-225.

49. J. Donahue, *Trial,* 58-63, for complete listing of intercalations and discussion of their significance.

50. E. Best, *Following Jesus,* 134-145.

51. J. Gnilka is typical of many commentators who place the whole section under the theology of the cross. He designates 8:27-10:45 as "Aufforderung zur Kreuzesnachfolge" in *Das Evangelium nach Markus* (EKK, II; Zürich; Einsiedeln, Köln: Benzinger; Neukirchen-Vluyn: Neukirchener Verlag, 1979) 2. 9.

52. H. Fleddermann, "The Discipleship Discourse (Mark 9:33-50)," *CBQ* 43 (1981) 60-61.

53. H.-W. Kuhn, *Altere Sammlungen im Markusevangelium* (SUNT, 8; Göttingen: Vandenhoeck und Ruprecht, 1971) 168-191; R. Pesch, *Markusevangelium,* 2. 128-130.

54. Examples from Q: Lk 14:25-26 = Mt 10:37-38; Lk 12:49-53 = Mt 10:34-35; Lk 9:57-62 = Mt 8:18-22.

55. *Sociology of Early Palestinian Christianity* (Philadelphia: Fortress, 1977) 8-16. Though, as I note, Mark may know of these traditions, he has a favorable view of "settled life." See 1:29-30 (Jesus enters home of Peter and heals Peter's mother-in-law); 2:12; 5:19; 8:26 (healed people are sent to their homes); 6:10 (itinerant disciples are to stay in a home); Jesus defends marriage (10:1-11) and the reception of children (9:36-37; 10:13-16). In Theissen's categories Mark would represent also the traditions of the "sympathizers in the local communities", 17-23.

56. E. Best, *Following Jesus,* 114; H.-J. Klauck, *Hausgemeinde,* 58-59.

57. For the wider context of such perspectives see, E. Schüssler-Fiorenza, "The Biblical Roots for the Discipleship of Equals," *Duke Divinity School Review* 45 (1980) 87-97, " 'You are not to be called Father.' Early Christian History in a Feminist Perspective," *Cross Currents* 29 (1979) 301-323, and "Discipleship and Patriarchy: Early Christian Ethos and Christian Ethics in a Feminist Theological Perspective," *The Annual of the Society of Christian Ethics,* 1982 (ed. L. Rasmussen; Dallas, TX: Perkins School of Theology, 1982) 131-172.

58. *The Sword of His Mouth* (Semeia Supplements, 1; Philadelphia: Fortress; Missoula: Scholars Press, 1975) 147-152.

59. R. Pesch, *Markusevangelium,* 2. 267, calls ch. 13 the most topical chapter of Mark's work.

60. *Home for the Homeless,* 165-237.

61. A. Berger, "patria potestas," *Oxford Classical Dictionary* (M. Cary *et al.,* eds.; Oxford: Clarendon Press, 1964) 653-654; "marriage," *Ibid.,* 539-540.

62. S. Benko, "Pagan Criticism of Christianity During the First Two Centuries," in *Aufstieg und Niedergang der römischen Welt* (ed. W. Haase; Berlin/New York: de Gruyter, 1980) 23. 1065.

63. P. Keresztes, "The Imperial Roman Government and the Christian Church. I. From Nero to the Servii," *Ibid.,* 215.

64. Marcus Cornelius Fronto (c. 100-166), cited by Minucius Felix (fl. c. 200-240) in Octavius, 8-9 (text as in Benko, "Pagan Criticism," 1082.

65. R. Pesch, *Markusevangelium,* 2. 159-160.

66. H. Beyer, *TDNT,* 2. 82.

67. IQS 6:2-7.

68. N. Perrin, "The Creative Use of the Son of Man Traditions by Mark," in *A Modern Pilgrimage in New Testament Christology* (Philadelphia: Fortress, 1974) 84-93.

69. The literature on Mk 10:45 is vast, see R. Pesch, *Markusevangelium,* 2. 166-167. In a recent study ("Salvation Proclaimed VII. Mark 10[45]: A Ransom for Many," *ExpTim* 93 [1982] 292-295) B. Lindars holds that Mark combines the ransom saying and the Son of Man saying and "holds together the two themes of service and sacrificial death which it [the preceding sequence] contains" (295).

70. D. E. Nineham, *Saint Mark* (Pelican Gospel Commentaries; Baltimore: Penguin, 1963) 358: "This [13:28-37] consists of a number of originally separate sayings and parables included here because they all deal with the general theme of watchfulness in view of the end."

71. W. Kelber, (*Kingdom,* 45-66) shows how Jesus' journeys to gentile territory anticipate the gentile mission.

72. J. Donahue, "A Neglected Factor," 578-581.

73. Col 3:18-4:1 *(Haustafel),* 1 Tim 2:8-15; 5:1-6:2; 1 Pet 2:13-3:7 *(Haustafel).* My comments here touch on two complex issues: (1) the nature and function of the NT "household codes" *(Haustafel)* and (2) the problem of "early Catholicism" or the institutionalization of the primitive Christian ethos. For the former see, J. Elliott, *Home for the Homeless,* 208-220; for the latter, D. Harrington, "The 'Early Catholic' Writings of the New Testament: The Church Adjusting to World History," in his *Light of All Nations: Essays on the Church in New Testament Research* (Wilmington, DE: Michael Glazier, 1982) 61-78.

74. Hugh Kenner, *The Pound Era,* 39, as cited in D. Crossan, *In Parables* (New York: Harper and Row, 1973) 2.

The Pere Marquette Theology Lectures

1969: "The Authority for Authority,"
by Quentin Quesnell
Professor of Theology at
Marquette University

1970: "Mystery and Truth,"
by John Macquarrie
Professor of Theology at
Union Theology Seminary, New York

1971: "Doctrinal Pluralism,"
by Bernard Lonergan, S.J.
Professor of Theology at
Regis College, Ontario

1972: "Infallibility,"
by George A. Lindbeck
Professor of Theology at
Yale University

1973: "Ambiguity in Moral Choice,"
by Richard A. McCormick, S.J.
Professor of Moral Theology at
Bellarmine School of Theology

1974: "Church Membership as a Catholic
and Ecumenical Problem,"
by Avery Dulles, S.J.
Professor of Theology at
Woodstock College

1975: "The Contributions of Theology to
Medical Ethics,"
by James Gustafson
University Professor of Theological Ethics at
University of Chicago

1976: "Religious Values in an Age of Violence,"
by Rabbi Marc Tanenbaum
Director of National Interreligious Affairs
American Jewish Committee, New York City

Uniform format, cover, and binding.

Copies of this Lecture and the others in the series
are obtainable from:

Marquette University Press
Marquette University
Milwaukee, Wisconsin 53233, U.S.A.

Publishers of:
- Mediaeval
  Philosophical
  Texts in Translations
- Père Marquette
  Theology Lectures
- St. Thomas
  Aquinas Lectures